Gaku's Question:

How Can Everyday People Create Peace?

108 Global Responses for Creating Peace Every Day

by

Betsy Johnston

Gaku's Question : How Can Everday People Create Peace? 108 Global Responses for Creating Peace Every Day.

For information contact : betsy.johnston.j@gmail.com

Cover art and design by Kaitlin Webb, kaitlinwebbart.com

Back page art by Gail Brown

ISBN: 9798640478709

First Edition: May 2020

10 9 8 7 6 5 4 3 2 1

Reviews of Gaku's Question:

"What an inspirational book! This is not a book to be read quickly, but rather to let each page marinate for a while. It is about being intentional about the goal of peace and how we can work toward it daily." – *Martha Krein, Elementary School Teacher for 38 years, Gillette, Wyoming*

"The beautiful thing about this book is that it reminds us that we can all work together to foster a world of peace. Regardless of age or where you are in your journey of life, by creating peace from within we can transform our lives, and the world around us. It was remarkable how connected I felt with the collective community brought together in these pages and reminded that everyday people can create peace. As you read through this book, you'll notice yourself becoming much more peaceful, relaxed, and hopeful about life. When we seek peace, peace becomes available! This book is a gift beyond measure." - *Pat Kilgannon, Executive Coach and Leadership Strategist, Doylestown, Pennsylvania*

"The author shares with the reader the fruits of a simple idea inspired by a young boy's question. Drawing on the collective wisdom of a larger community, she has brought together voices sharing pathways to peace. We see from the contributors to "Gaku's Question" that peace is created by the decisions and action of everyday people. This collection of work, offering up insights from our neighbors, children, and the global community is a reminder that peace is embedded in the details and choices of everyday life. So, ask your children, your friends, your neighbors Gaku's question. Imagine the conversation that might follow. In their world, in their imaginations and in their responses, you also may find humanity's path forward - many small, selfless suggestions in service to a better world. "Gaku's Question" reinforces what we already know in our human hearts full of an endless capacity for love. Peace begins with me. - *Nancy Cornwell, Ph.D., Professor Film & Photography, Montana State University, Bozeman, Montana*

How Can Everyday People Create Peace?

DEDICATION:

❖ *to Gaku*, for asking the question first,
❖ *to my mother, Jean Johnston*, who believes that everyone has at least one book to write,
❖ *to my three beautiful children, Sarah, Kaitlin and Parker*, who are each creating peace in their own ways.

> *Imagine all the people living life in peace,*
> *You may say I'm a dreamer*
> *But I'm not the only one...*
> **John Lennon**

THE PREMISE

It was September 2017 and I was sitting on the floor enjoying an incredible meal in Northern Japan during a visit to my friend who was teaching English there. The atmosphere, the array of tasty dishes, and the hosts were warm and inviting. Gaku, their 13-year old son, sat on the floor close to me and had many questions about the work I was doing related to non-violent conflict management in several countries in Africa. He pulled out maps to see where I had been working and where my travels had led. At the time, North Korean leader Kim Jong-un was testing missiles that were flying over their town in the trajectory. His eyes on mine, Gaku leaned in, grinned, and asked, *"How can everyday people create peace?"* This question, asked by a 13-year old boy, is the source of this collection of responses.

As a facilitator by profession, instead of answering the question myself, I posed it back to him. *"How can everyday people create peace?"* Gaku's 13 year-old response is the first in this collection. I asked him again at age 16, and it is the last in this collection.

I am fortunate to travel both for work and for play, and over the last few years, I have asked this question of different people, of differing ages, genders, ethnicities and nationalities. I asked the question on buses, on trains, on planes, on bar stools, in classrooms, while walking el Camino de Santiago Frances, and on the streets of the villages in which I traveled. The youngest contributor was Gako at age 13 and the oldest contributor is my mother at age 94. Forty countries from around the globe are represented here.

You will discover themes about kindness and about peace starting from within. Many of the responses include self-responsibility for creating peace in our everyday lives. Writings by the younger contributors inspire me – these youth believe in peace and maintain hope for the future. And, they know what individual action can do.

In 2017, I volunteered for two weeks at the Liger Leadership Academy in Cambodia teaching communication and conflict management skills to a group of bright future leaders. You will read their responses scattered throughout. I am also a faculty member teaching civic engagement and project management through the Middle Eastern Partnership Initiative. Student leaders from North Africa and the Middle East come to the USA to learn about leadership and effecting change. Many of the MENA region responses come from these inspiring students. My sister-in-law teaches high school on a reservation in western Montana and her student responses are a result of her creative writing work with them.

The 108 responses do not appear in any specific order. I chose the sacred number 108, representing the wholeness of existence, connecting science with the human mind, body and spirit. In yoga, 108 sun salutations are practiced to honor change – for example, to bring peace, respect and understanding at a time of global uncertainty.

I added a daily intention following each contribution to offer specific ideas of how individuals can foster peace. These are offered only as suggestions - feel free to assign your own intentions to what you read.

I designed, collated and edited this collection during the 2020 Covid19 global health crisis. The contributions helped me with the uncertainty, powerlessness, fear, and grief that came with the virus. As I brought the collection together, I felt like I was able to visit again with each contributor. I thank them for their words of wisdom and hope during uncertain times.

I hope you are also inspired by the responses to Gaku's question and guided to cultivate peace in your own life. My yoga teacher, Lilly, ends each practice with *"May you make peace with the past, live in peace in the present, and cultivate peace in the future."*
Namaste, BJJ

*May you make peace with the past,
live in peace in the present,
and cultivate peace in the future.*

1. Gaku, 13, Japan

"I think that you have to listen really well. And smiling helps. And you have a really nice smile…"

Today's Intention: I will listen without distractions to one person whom I encounter today. I will show I am listening with my smile.

2. Sreynith, 17, Cambodia

"If you are unsatisfied with someone, you should immediately try to solve the problem with that person (quick action on solving a problem).

Today's intention: If I find myself in a conflict today (big or small), I will use my voice to problem-solve with the other and not wait until another day.

3. Yarinett, 35, Venezuela

"I believe that Peace comes from inside you! As long as you feel Peace in your mind, your heart and your soul you will spread Peace around you.

------Peace as a consequence of love, gratitude, sharing and care!-----"

Today's intention: At the end of this day I feel peace because I have paused to feel gratitude and I have expressed love for someone in my life.

As the world fights to figure everything out, I'll be holding doors for strangers, letting people cut in front of me in traffic, saying good morning, keeping babies entertained in grocery lines, stopping to talk to someone who is lonely, being patient with sales clerks, smiling at passersby. WHY? Because I will not stand idly by and live in a world where love is invisible. Join me in showing kindness, understanding, and judging less. Be kind to a stranger, give grace to friends who are having a bad day, be forgiving of yourself - today and every day. BE the change, BE the light, start today and never stop.
Audrey L Pary

4. Arik, 33, South Sudan

"Learning to shut down our own biases about others is one of the most difficult things to do. However, if people are kind enough to increase awareness of their insensitivity towards others and keep in check their stereotypical behavior before it escalates to other levels of hate, I believe everyday people will create peace."

Today's intention: Today I will commit to learning more about my own biases and stereotypes. I will have a conversation with a friend, do research online, check a book out of the library, or ask a local non-profit for education opportunities.

5. Amira, 23, Tunisia

"I believe that promoting peace starts from within. Inner peace comes from knowing your beliefs and the willingness to act according to them. Indeed, this would ultimately enlighten your knowledge about the fact that we are all different and that we should accept and respect others regardless of their beliefs. Thus, this would create a peaceful realm where everybody can live together."

Today's intention: I will write down 2 values that are important to me. Throughout my day, I will align my behavior with my values.

6. Ali, 23, Libya

"Whenever the word 'peace' comes to my mind, I directly correlate it with other aspects in life which cannot be achieved without it. Such as equality, justice & freedom. As a young person who lives in one of the most dangerous territories in the world, I keep reminding myself of these values every moment during my everyday struggles, and even if we didn't acquire any of it yet, I feel that it's really worth fighting for. Peace will happen if every one of us respected each other's freedom of choice, speech, and beliefs, along with accepting diversity, and showing more tolerance toward our differences."

Today's intention: Today, I will be tolerant and respectful of someone with a different point of view than my own. I will listen to them with an open-mind to better understand them.

> *Traditionally, it's taught that patience is the antidote to aggression.*
> **Pema Chodron**

7. George, 54, Greece/South Africa

"They must be more patient. Patience will bring the rest. And that is my answer to your question."

Today's intention: I will take a deep breath and stay present, even if I want to rush or push through something today – a traffic light, waiting in line, waiting for a response, or helping a child.

8. Beecham, 35 Uganda

"Peace starts with joy and humility that we possess within the deepest of our hearts towards the life and blessings around us."

Today's intention: I will notice a moment when I feel joy and I will pause to feel the blessing and gratitude that accompanies it.

9. Hamza, 34, Morocco

"Looking at world conflicts can engender an overwhelming feeling of hopelessness and despair, but despite all of that, everyday people can indeed create peace. One can start with spreading awareness in their local community and learning about the tools needed in order to manage a conflict. We can all create peace by acknowledging our limited capacity to how much we can do. Both empathy and kindness can push us towards actions that contribute to peace creation."

Today's intention: I will ask someone today how they managed a recent conflict. I will take note of what skills they used and what they learned from the conflict.

10. Chhoeu, 17, Cambodia

"Always be the scale – balance both sides and find a middle point. Always be calm and be open. Control yourself, calm before the storm! Look and listen, then think before saying! Peace in yourself – learn, who are we really? Fight against the tormentors by encouraging the tormented to not be silent but to be hopeful. Train our brains to be positive!"

Today's intention: Today I will think before I speak, considering if what I am going to say will lead to greater understanding or into a win/lose debate. I will use my voice for positive problem-solving.

11. Karen, 57, Denmark

"Smile. You can communicate peace to others non-verbally. Smile and start a connection."

Today's intention: I will communicate peace through my body language. Twice during the day I will stop and reflect about how I convey this.

In our daily life we can smile, if we can be peaceful and happy, not only we, but everyone will profit from it. This is the most basic kind of peace work.
Thich Nhat Hahn

12. Nora, 22, Morocco

"The fear of the unknown is the main cause of many international conflicts our world is facing. This fear creates a lack of respect and tolerance to our unique differences. Thus, traveling for me is our great opportunity to create peace. When I travel, I discover/understand new cultures, enlighten myself and people around me with history, geography and inspirational stories. We create peace everyday by working toward strengthening the wonders of our cultural diversities and embracing our differences."

Today's intention: If I cannot travel somewhere new, I will travel virtually. I will research a new country, a new cultural tradition, or a new language.

13. Therese, 38, Australia

"First, smile. Make eye contact. Acknowledge each other. Keep smiling. It has to do with uniting. I don't like conflict, but I do like people. I wake up in the morning and want peace."

Today's intention: I will demonstrate my affection for people today by smiling and making eye contact.

Never worry about numbers. Help one person at a time, and always start with the person nearest you.
Mother Teresa

14. Ibtisam, 42, Jordan

"I think peace is a responsibility of every person. He should have peace inside his heart, then to wider level in his family by living and dealing with them peacefully. By doing this there will be no conflict because in the houses the process of building humans begins and kids learn how to not be greedy and violent. I hope my answer will help because really I hate the human's aggression and cruelty."

Today's intention: Today I will work to create peace in my family. I'll have a conversation with a family member and soothe a conflict by listening and accepting instead of judging or criticizing.

15. Maurice, 52, France/Thailand

"It is not because your country is not at war, that you are at peace in your daily life. Most people (around the world) struggle to get the basic means for themselves and closest relatives such as food and water, medicine, school. These are the pillars for family. When they have the basics they still have to think about other (extra) things like get a transport, pay for their clothes, electricity, etc... Once they have that they might be at peace in their mind at least..."

Today's intention: I will create a path to help those who do not have their basic needs met – donate clothes, donate food, donate time/resources to a NGO, volunteer at a food bank, or serve a meal at a shelter.

> *Taking the vow to help others implies that instead of holding our own individual territory and defending it tooth and nail, we become open to the world that we are living in. It means we are willing to take on greater responsibility, immense responsibility. In fact, it means taking a big chance.*
> **Chogyam Trungpa Rinpoche**

16. Soliday, 17, Cambodia

"Personally, I think peace is something that is inside every one of us. Its difference depends on each individual because we define and look for peace in different ways depending upon our situations. To promote peace sounds like promoting a product, but as we think about it, it is as simple as practicing our daily life. Sharing love is as simple a concept as I can think of. Being able to care, to be kind and friendly, to create relationships, is something everyone can do because peace is a part of happiness and contentment and affection. It's hard for some people to find peace because they have feared in their lives. So being able to understand and acknowledge your own fear can lead to creating peace. Confront your fear instead of avoiding it."

Today's intention: I will reflect on what makes me afraid. How do feelings of fear interfere with creating peace in my life?

17. Joan, 73, USA

"We all have the ability to reach out to our friends and share information on what is hindering the less fortunate in our community. Then we do research on how to remedy the problem that interests us the most whether it is transportation, food security or health care. The organizations that are helping with these problems can always use physical and/or financial help. Volunteering is not always understood in many cultures but it is always easier to affect change with the help of a critical mass of concerned friends rather than alone.

Today's intention: I will donate my time or money to an organization that helps people in my community.

18. Chimean, 18, Cambodia

"Create graciousness not violence."

Today's intention: When I feel anger growing inside me, I will breathe in the anger and breathe out peace. I will acknowledge the feeling and prepare to listen.

We will not learn how to live together in peace by killing each other's children.
Jimmy Carter

19. Richmond, 31, Ghana/USA

"First, everyday people can create peace by seeing and treating each other irrespective of our differences (natural or humanmade) as humans. From my observation, the absence of either internal or external peace (sometimes both) is a result of our attitude towards others. Second, we can create peace by respecting nature. The environment serves us our 'home;' we wouldn't have peace if we continue to destroy the source of our existence. Nature will either react or give up. Each of these can have some serious consequences for a peaceful world."

Today's intention: I will do one thing today that helps the environment – for example, walking instead of driving, buying with an eye to packaging, or reusing instead of throwing out.

20. Gary, 60, Scotland

"Not be belligerent."

Today's intention: As I move through this day, I will consider my responses to others, in-person and on social media. Instead of crafting angry or mean-spirited responses to those with whom I disagree, I will choose thoughtfulness.

So war and peace start in the human heart. Whether that heart is open or whether that heart is closed has global implications.
Pema Chodron

21. Rajesh, 35, India

"One could create peace everyday by being conscious that it is natural to get angry when mistreated by others. Sometimes we wrongly perceive anger as maltreatment as we are hardwired to believe only ourselves are free of mistake-making behaviour. Also keeping in mind what Gandhiji said is helpful, 'An eye for an eye will make the world blind.' We tend to become worse than our enemy while taking revenge - something which also happens when we retaliate. So this cycle of violence becomes self-perpetuating."

Today's intention: When I feel angry, I will acknowledge the angry feeling instead of making a hurtful comment or striking back. By not retaliating, I'll stop the cycle of violence.

22. Rathanak, 17, Cambodia

"In order to remain at peace, we should show our kindness, respect, help, and to ensure rights for every individual.

- *Kindness: keep smiling at each other.*
- *Respect: listening and accepting each decision.*
- *Help: seeking opportunities to help each other.*
- *Ensure rights for every individual: provide rights for each other in making decisions."*

Today's intention: Today I will take one action to support the rights of others. I will show up as an ally for basic human rights like gender equity, freedom of religion, and freedom of speech.

23. Denise, 58, Australia

"Be kind. You don't know what others are going through. It's simple, be bloody kind."

Today's intention: I will pause to consider the ways I can show kindness today. Through simple acts – let someone in front of me, smile, offer to carry a bag, check on an elderly neighbor.

> *There are three ways to ultimate success: The first way is to be kind. The second way is to be kind. The third way is to be kind.*
> **Fred Rogers**

24. Ron, 68, USA

"Creating peace requires changing hearts. Growing up I was a very angry young man. Getting into fights was pretty common. Bouncing from relationship to relationship was also common. As I matured, I came to grips with the physical abuse I suffered as a child at the hands of my father while my mother looked on and did nothing. It took decades to reconcile and forgive but it happened. That day I fully understood my dad's PTSD from being in three invasions in World War II and seeing his friends killed is a burden he carried all his life.

The point is that true individual peace for myself which, by the way, was also an advantage to my own family, came when I forgave. I forgave my dad for the abuse. I forgave my mom who stood by and watched, helpless. How did I recognize this inner peace? I found myself as the main caregiver for my parents as they aged and passed within 19 months of one another due to Alzheimer's. I held their hands as they took their final breaths. I prayed with them. I told them I loved them. Holding their hands as they passed changed me. The experience changed me for the better. It made me a better husband, father, and person for others. I found individual peace through forgiveness."

Today's intention: Today I will forgive my family of origin for the pain that I experienced as a child. I will put the old burdens down and express my love.

25. Seyah, 18, Cambodia

"Follow the nature of Gandhi. Treat every day as if it is your last day and give it all you've got. Use your heart and understand logic before instinct. Care and love for others even if unrelated, no matter who they are."

Today's intention: I will travel through this day with my heart and my eyes wide open.

Be kind; Everyone you meet is fighting a hard battle.
John Watson

26. Nakai, 27, Cayman Islands

"Everyday people can create peace by treating one another with respect and kindness. That can be done easily by saying 'Good Morning,' 'Good Afternoon' or 'Evening' when you pass by people as you are walking down the street, heading home, etc. A few other ways are to respect other people's privacy. Helping one another is another way, whether it's opening a door for someone, assisting elders to cross streets or with groceries. Being truthful is one of the most important ways to having peace. Yes the truth can hurt, but it will show that honesty is there and therefore help the issue."

Today's intention: I will speak the truth, even if it is uncomfortable, modeling honesty as a personal value.

27. Steve, 62, USA

"Perhaps the best way one person can bring world peace is to be a catalyst for peace. Help your elderly neighbor with their garden, hold a door for someone you don't know, or maybe be happy and positive. These simple acts will be seen by others and possibly stir them to start bringing more peace and happiness in their own way."

Today's intention: I will practice one random act of kindness today with a friend, family member, neighbor, or a stranger.

"Oh, "she says, "well, you're not a poor man. You know, why don't you go online and buy a hundred envelopes and put them in the closet?" And so I pretend not to hear her. And go out to get an envelope because I'm going to have a hell of a good time in the process of buying one envelope. I meet a lot of people. And see some great looking babies. And a fire engine goes by. And I give them the thumbs up. And I'll ask a woman what kind of dog that is. And, I don't know. The moral of the story is – we're here on Earth to fart around. And, of course, the computers will do us out of that. And what the computer people don't realize, or they don't care, is we're dancing animals. You know, we love to move around. And it's like we're not supposed to dance at all anymore.

Kurt Vonnegut

28. David, 17, Cambodia

"Freedom of speech – many people are afraid of speaking out loud of things that they don't agree on and the silence slowly strikes their hearts. People have fear to speak out loud because they know if they do many people may dislike their idea and people will put them outside of the circle. If all places practice freedom of speech it will help people to come up with solutions that fit most of them."

Today's intention: I will invite differing points of view into my circle. I will encourage others to speak up by listening deliberately.

29. Hachem, 23, Morocco

"I believe that with a positive mindset whilst being less selfish, everyday people can create peace. Simple actions like caring for each other could help us move forward: individually minor, but collectively significant."

Today's intention: I will impact my community today with my positive attitude and through one simple action initiated by me to another.

30. Jaci, 63, USA

"When I think of the idea of world peace, I remember myself as a scared 6-year-old, sheltering under a desk during a bomb drill. In the decades following WWII and as the war in Vietnam was escalating, the fear was so great in our country that we had bomb drills in the 1960's at Rattlesnake Elementary in Missoula. Even though the U.S. mainland has never been invaded by a foreign country, the idea of war has been with me all these years. How do we create peace? It has to start within and when we are at peace, we can project it to the world through the way we treat others."

Today's intention: I will practice peace within by sitting quietly for 10 minutes and visualizing treating others peacefully for the rest of the day.

She asks me to kill the spider. Instead, I get the most peaceful weapons I can find. I take a cup and a napkin. I catch the spider, put it outside and allow it to walk away. If I am every caught in the wrong place at the wrong time, just being alive and not bothering anyone, I hope I am greeted with the same kind of mercy.
Rudy Francisco

31. Neang, 17, Cambodia

"Peace can be promoted by actions that are being displayed by someone like:

- *Accepting: forgive and forget what happened*
- *Listening: to other people's thoughts*
- *Giving people the right to speak up regardless of their age, gender, or social status*
- *Not forcing people to do what they don't want to do, yet show them what's right and what's wrong*
- *Peace is not physically attacking others to get rid of conflicts, yet is about settling down problems in a calm manner*
- *Peace is not about ignoring problems, yet is about facing the problems and dealing with them*

·   *Give time for people to make up their minds before sorting out problems"*

Today's intention: I will take the necessary time to resolve a problem with another, facing it directly and calmly.

How lovely to think that no one need wait a moment. We can start now, start slowly, changing the world. How lovely that everyone, great and small, can make a contribution toward introducing justice straightaway. And we can always, always give something, even if it is only kindness!
Anne Frank

32. Martin, 57, Sweden

"I think you've already got the answer. Smiling leads to peace."

Today's intention: I will consider the way I appear to others. Do I present a welcoming posture, do I smile, am I relaxed and open to engagement? How do I represent a peaceful demeanor?

33. Andy, 60, USA

"It's simple for everyday people to create peace. Give yourself into helping others and really live it. Have compassion. Be happy. Peace will come..."

Today's intention: Today I commit to choosing a way to volunteer in my community. If I can't volunteer today, I will choose a local group to call to inquire about volunteering to get started.

34. Makara, 17, Cambodia

"There are five different ways that I believe people can do to promote peace. First of all, confronting. We need to deal with conflict. If we don't do it, it means that we are creating an environment that is full of misgivings because we know this problem will occur in the future. Secondly, we should be open-minded because every person is different. So, we need to listen to everyone's perspective before making a decision. There are 3 other ways: empathy; get help when seeing violence against other people or when you feel unsafe; learn from different conflicts – so that we are not following down the same path or so we can learn from how peace happens (and apply to our life)."

Today's intention: I will research the resources available in my community for helping victims of violence. I will learn who to call for help if I witness violence or if I am feeling unsafe.

35. Paz, 43, USA/Philippines

"There are many ways everyday people can create peace - it is an intentional practice to avoid assuming the intentions of others, to choose to respond with kindness to those who may mistreat us, and to acknowledge and take responsibility for our role in conflict or hurt. It is easier to play to role of victim, especially in the hyper-reactionary culture that I live in, but I find it is more satisfying and human to play an active part in my surroundings. If I can put positive energy into the world, not only does it bring peace to my heart, but it hopefully is spread to others as well."

Today's intention: When I find myself in conflict with another, I will consider what assumptions I am making about their intentions and what stories I am making up about the situation. I will take responsibility for my role within the conflict.

36. Sreyneang, 17, Cambodia

"Pick up life example like genocide, to show the comparison of living with family, with freedom, having your own choice, no pressure. In addition to this we need people to understand what others have faced during times of genocide like Khmer Rouge. In conversations with kids or adults ask them if they feel the peace surrounding them. Then, bring them into the situation of war/genocide/violence. Which then shows the result of lost and not-peaceful. After, not just showing the experience to be scared of, but pushes them into a different direction in a positive way that could bring peace. Share examples of peace in their daily life, society and world. We should give them time to create a story from documenting peace that came from wars to bring non-violent action."

Today's intention: I will educate myself about the history of genocide and the conditions that contribute to genocide.

37. Andrea, 47, Slovakia/Ireland

"Kindness. To all others and to yourself. It has to start with yourself and go on from there."

Today's intention: I will show kindness to myself today.

When we start to develop maitri for ourselves, unconditional acceptance of ourselves, then we're really taking care of ourselves in a way that pays off. We feel more at home with our own bodies and minds and more at home in the world. As our kindness for ourselves grows, so does our kindness for other people.
Pema Chodron

38. Sarah, 29, USA

"Everyday people can create peace through empathy. Through empathy -- an every day deliberate attempt to see issues, experiences, or human responses from a multitude of different perspectives, cultures, and religions -- humankind can create meaningful connections, free of judgement. Peace does not require agreement, consensus, or conformity to the same idea or to a specific mantra; but rather, a deliberate attempt to recognize the innate humanity in another person.

Peace requires that humankind around the globe make a deliberate attempt to consider ideas from a new angle, ask questions to better understand one another, and take comfort in knowing that we are not all the same. Peace requires an appreciation of diversity, divergent thinking, and perspectives that push our own assumptions or values. To create peace, everyday people must first strive to create empathy."

Today's intention: Rather than share what I know, today I will ask questions and learn from others.

39. Melissa, 21, Algeria

"I believe the answer to how can everyday people create peace is by finding it within themselves first. Once we understand what we are and embrace our inner persona, we can accept everyone else's. Isn't the greatest suffering caused by not understanding and accepting each other? It is simply because we are afraid of differences, we don't know how to deal with them, so we go on destroying the beautiful human bond between us instead of restoring it. And to restore it, we have to stand out with our own pieces and our own uniqueness so the world can see it and do the same. All so different, but all the same."

Today's intention: Today I will acknowledge something unique about myself and look outside myself to honor something unique about another.

40. Rithy, 17, Cambodia

"Everyone should have the same amount of rights. No judgement of the poor by the wealthy classes. Everyone should show their love to their surrounding people. Education could create peace because when people get a standard education it means they will have the ability to find good jobs. So that everyone is happy to live without social classes and judgment.

Today's Intention: Today I will ask myself how I support education in my community. Voting, volunteering, participating? What responsibility do I have in the education of people in my community?

41. Viktoria, 23, Russia/Germany

"To start with themselves. Create peace within themselves. What you feel inside will influence people outside. It will affect the people around you. If you see the world as peaceful, you will resolve the conflicts in that way."

Today's intention: I will sit in meditation for 10 minutes this morning, creating the calm and peace I want to carry with me through the day.

The only way to bring peace to the earth is to learn to make our own life peaceful.
Buddha

42. Leyth, 21, Tunisia

"One simple way of creating peace in the world is promoting empathy and applying it in every one of our daily encounters. Putting ourselves in the other's shoes allows not only to understand their perspective, and thus their actions and the reasoning behind it, but it also makes them feel understood. This creates harmonious relationships, reduces stress, and enhances emotional awareness, allowing for mutual understanding and lower chances of conflict. Feeling misunderstood is one of the hardest burdens to bear. It often leads to loneliness and alienation, which are a fertile terrain for cultivating hatred. If we all try to be more empathetic towards others, the world would probably become a more peaceful place."

Today's intention: Who in my community might be feeling misunderstood, lonely or alienated? Today my mantra will be empathy and my intent will be to put myself in another's shoes.

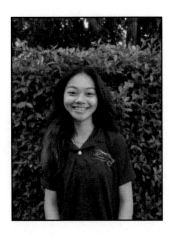

43. Souyeth, 17, Cambodia

"Take courage to say 'sorry' or 'I forgive you.' It's like when your nails get longer. You don't cut the finger, you just cut the nail. The same thing with arguments. You cut your ego, not the relationship. Sometimes you have to give up pride, so you and the other person can solve the problem."

Today's intention: Would I rather be right or happy? Today I will set aside my ego and take the time to apologize or forgive someone with whom I have a conflict.

44. Julian, 18, USA

"Peace comes within
Peace is found inside
Outside is an unknown
an un-welcomed source
Peace can be gained
Peace is achievable
Peace is one
Peace can be changed from outside
Outside is a cold hard reality
But Taming that reality is what
Peace is"

Today's intention: I will reflect on where I think peace begins.
Inside, outside, or both? Where can I have the biggest impact?

45. Mohammed, 21, Algeria

"Since I was a child, I have been urged to spread peace between people. For me, it is by respecting everyone, regardless of our opinions or orientations, because difference makes distinction. The human being is peaceful and if you want to confirm that you can notice how children treat each other, so why not try being a child for the rest of your life?"

Today's intention: What messages about peace did I learn from society as a child? How did my parents teach me about resolving conflicts? Today I will reflect on how these messages and lessons shape the way I experience peace.

46. Oliver, 23, Rwanda

"How everyday people create peace:
1) Peace comes from being humble,
2) Connecting with your neighbor,
3) Love each other."

Today's intention: I will connect with one of my neighbors today and I will offer help or support if needed.

47. Katina, 63, USA

"Dear sweet Gaku, How can an everyday person create peace? As an everyday person in this world I BELIEVE in PEACE. I BREATHE PEACE. I WALK IN PEACE. I CONNECT WITH OTHERS PEACEFULLY. I LIVE FULLY IN PEACE. Saint seraphim writes, 'Acquire a SPIRIT OF PEACE........ and a thousand souls are lifted!' What an amazing ripple effect. This empowers me so that when I get down, I CHOOSE to reconnect with INTERNAL PEACE! Because I desire peace and joy in me and in this world. I know that my internal state of being affects every one of my cells in my body. And then it spreads out like a pebble in the pond."

Today's intention: What kind of ripple effect do my emotions have on others? Calming, peaceful, angry, critical? Today I will intentionally choose the ripple effect I want to have on others.

We look forward to the time when the Power of Love will replace the Love of Power. Then will our world know the blessings of peace.
William Ewart Goldstone

48. June & Sookhee, 60 & 65, South Korea

June says, *"I have to make peace with my wife first. And, you must support peace from the inside, it's called 'rejo' in Korean. I pray for peace. There is nothing more you can do."* Sookhee was hesitant to answer, she added, *"Just what he says."*

Today's intention: I will consider how I create peace in my own home. In what ways do I resolve conflict to strengthen relationships or engage with a partner to build peace together?

49. Susi, 37, Tirol/Austria

"As soon as people start being grateful for everything they have in their life, and as soon as they stop envying others for what they have - people create peace around them and among them. Greed and envy are poison, both emotions lead to hate and frustration ... so, understanding that other people's success and fortune, their friends, their job etc. might not even be right for you - as it is their life not yours - and understanding that whatever you've created for yourself is good just the way it is, is the first step towards a grateful, fulfilling and most of all peaceful life...for you and everyone around you..."

Today's intention: I will name 2 things I am grateful for today. I will express gratitude for these things in my life as I move throughout the day.

50. Samady, 18, Cambodia

"Everyone has the potential to bring peace and freedom to their nation or surroundings, but it takes time and effort to do it. You don't have to be the most powerful person in order to make change, you just need compassion, determination, and passion to do it. One individual can bring peace by doing something that is non-violent. This would influence the others to not get into a fight when having conflict. Both needed to find a way that both could come into an agreement, it's like compromising. If there is conflict around one, then one should help solve the problems to prevent it from getting bigger. In your community, if you want to promote peace, you could create a project to tell more people about peace. Do simple things such as: forgive, smile, show compassion, think positive, understand each other, compromise/accommodate."

Today's intention: Today I will practice compromising by meeting someone in the middle to come to an agreement.

She felt like doing her part to change the world, so she started by giving thanks for all the blessings in her life, rather than bemoaning all that was missing from it. Then she complimented her reflection in the mirror instead of criticizing it as she usually did. Next she walked into her neighborhood and offered her smile to everyone she passed, whether or not they offered theirs to her. Each day she did these things and soon they became habit. Each day she lived with more gratitude, more acceptance, more kindness. And sure enough, the World around her began to change. Because she had decided so, she was single-handedly doing her part to change it.
Scott Stabile

51. Martin, 66, USA

"Before I can answer that question, I need to answer the question, what is peace? I believe it is the lack of conflict; if so, what is conflict? I believe it is a separation between people where one is no longer able to see the other in living life. To close this gap, we must strive as individuals to be whole with all of created beings. We need to pause and see the common light that flows through everything and to consciously enter into oneness with that light. It is in that instance where it is not possible to be separate, to be in conflict...we are at peace."

Today's intention: I will see the divine in others as I move through the day. The light in me acknowledges and honors the light in you.

52. Kawtar, 21, Morocco

"A person is peaceful when he decides to mind his own business, when he invests his time working on himself not underestimating others and when he doesn't mind to co-exist with people of a different background than his own, because he loves and believes in diversity. And if he ever thinks he's unable to do good to his surroundings, he at least forbids himself of doing them any harm."

Today's intention: I will do no harm to others today.

53. AudriAnna, 18, USA

*"This is unfortunate for me to say,
but there will never be world peace as long as
humans are around.
We have become a sort of angry, offended and
murderous compound.
Wars continue to plague our world year after
year.
We don't care if we kill and cause people's skin
to rip and tear.
We make innocent children constantly be
riddled with fear.
As kind, intelligent and respectable people are
becoming more and more rare.
As anger continues to grind inside us as if our
insides were like mashed pears.*

So as long as humans infect the world, peace shall never see the light of day.
Up until the day the last human begins to decay."

Today's intention: I will take note of when I feel anger in my body. I will breathe, remain calm, and make a conscious decision to be constructive.

54. Theara, 17, Cambodia

"We should not engage in violence. Treat everyone with kindness, love and respect. This shouldn't be based on gender, religion, skin color, etcetera. Moreover, develop meaningful relationships with them. Try to consider things from other's point of view because it will help you to understand their intentions and reasons. Provide help when someone is in trouble or needed."

Today's intention: I will treat everyone I encounter today with respect regardless of gender, religion, skin color, age, or dress.

55. Clark, 27, Canada

"Forgiveness – forgive self and others. At the end of the day, you get to make a choice between hating and forgiveness. You don't necessarily agree with the other person, but you let it go."

Today's intention: I will forgive someone for a conflict that I have held onto. I will let it go.

56. Sythong, 17, Cambodia

"Things people can do to promote peace: Spread love and empathy. Live in wisdom. Respect. Forgive and understand. This might take a long time until the surrounding people understand. But the more you show it, the more it melts a person and gets them to consider about peace."

Today's intention: What does "live in wisdom" mean to me? I will use the wisdom I already have inside me to guide my interactions with others towards peace today.

Be that one. That one who forgives when deep offense has been committed. That one who loves when no one else does. That one who gives kindness to those who are mean. Be that one who looks past the insult, instead seeing the pain that motivated it. That one who shines light upon those who sit in utter darkness. Because the impact of being that one runs far and wide. It brings healing to the wounded, joy to the sad, and hope to those in despair. Be that one.
Sheri Eckert

57. Sorcha, 24, Ireland

"Everyday people can create peace by striving to treat others the way they would like to be treated - by showing respect, compassion and kindness. It is important that we approach others with an open mind and that we make an effort to educate ourselves on different cultures and beliefs. By treating others in this way, we are positively creating peace and harmony and reducing the risk of conflict that can arise due to unkind action/words and prejudice."

Today's intention: I will move through this day treating others the way I wish to be treated.

58. Noriko, 59, Japan

"Have common sense with neighbors and behave as mature adults."

Today's intention: Instead of acting on impulse or ignoring the impact I have on others, I will choose to dialogue purposefully in the way I interact today.

59. Tika Ram, 49, Nepal

"Every day is unique and it brings a good fortune to us. But greed and jealousy deter us from peace of mind as it fuels our mind to negativity. If we have full faith on each other with a feeling of fraternity, I am pretty sure peace prevails there."

Today's intention: "Comparison is the thief of joy" (Theodore Roosevelt). Today I will consider the ways I allow comparison to affect my inner peace.

60. Doc, 61, USA

"Peace begins within the internal landscape of one's mind, body, heart, and spirit. To do the good work of becoming whole, where these elements are aligned is essential if we are going to seek out peace in our external world. It should be noted, however, that it is rare to arrive at a permanent state of peace. Life keeps upsetting our perfectly crafted plans and environments. This is ongoing work where we honor where we are at any given moment, including the shadows of our own souls that we often seek to keep divided from our light. To live a life of wholeness of being in a world that offers much strife and chaos is and always will be a great work-in-progress for as long as we *have breath.*

(1) Make the gifts of individuals visible and useful
(2) Self-organize around basic human principles of dignity and respect
(3) Learn to live simply, so they are not beholden to the handcuffs of large corporate tactics and greed
(4) Exchange good and services amongst members so that membership has life-giving benefits that bypass traditional good and services supply chains.
(5) Provide educational opportunities to practice win-win games that foster the spirit of abundance in their communities of practice.

Today's intention: What does living simply mean to me? In what ways can I simplify my life – possessions, commitments, scheduling, relationships? I will choose one action for the day that focuses on living simply.

61. Nilroth, 17, Cambodia

"A simple act of kindness makes an endless ripple. Always try to seek for situations where you can make a positive contribution. That small contribution will inspire others to contribute as well. Avoid using violence. When citizens don't use violence, the government would be so tilted if they use violence to solve conflicts. Show love to each other. Smile to strangers."

Today's intention: I will calmly use my voice and body language to model positive problem-solving, providing others with an example to follow for their response to conflict.

> Do not be daunted by the enormity of the world's grief. Do justly now. Love mercy now. Walk humbly now... you are not obligated to complete the work, but neither are you free to abandon it.
>
> **The Talmud**

62. Sam, 65, USA

"I strongly believe dialogue can bring about peace. I'm a practicing Buddhist, and member of the SGI USA Buddhist lay organization, which promotes Peace, Education and Culture. Quoting Dr. Susan H. Allen, 'When we look at it through a consciousness lens, we can see some of the magic of dialogue. We become more aware of others' perspectives, but we also become more aware of our own perspective. This awakened awareness can lead to a moment when shift happens, when our consciousness transitions from 'My way is the right way' to realizing, 'Oh, it's really complex; there are lots of factors here, and I can see where they're coming from.' "

Today's intention: I will explore the magic of dialogue, listening for others' perspectives and becoming more aware of my own. I will acknowledge that many factors contribute to the present situation.

63. Alae, 24, Morocco

"How can everyday people create peace? By interacting with each other, meeting new people, discovering new cultures and create strong and life lasting bonds with other people from the other corner of the world, with your fellow citizens and neighbors, but most importantly with yourself! Get to know yourself, have peace within your own self, your own family, your neighborhood and scale it up to the whole world. The peace our nations are trying to instill starts from within! Peace upon you!"

Today's intention: I will begin with peace in myself, within my family next , in my neighborhood, and then beyond.

64. Colleen, 56, England/France

"There are a couple of things. I think people should educate themselves and not take one source of information as fact. Cause you read it on Facebook doesn't mean it's true. But if you want to do something really dramatic, maybe we should all do exchange. So maybe I should allow a family in Somalia to come and live in my house and I should go and live in their house. And if we walked in other people's shoes, then we'd see more than their religion and the color of their skin. And actually see the conditions they were living in. And then maybe the guilt would make us all think we have to do something."

Today's intention: I will take time to understand truth of the media in an era of "fake news." I will verify the information I access through a variety of sources before passing it along to others.

65. Sreypich, 18, Cambodia

"Nature creates us to have love and pain and we might question why we need both. Every human has evil and good in themself and they need to learn to balance. To create peace, we should learn how to live with kindness, virtuousness and appreciate what is given. Your positivity and perspective can shape someone else's.

Today's intention: Today I will look at the balance between love and pain, good and evil, kindness and cruelty, joy and grief. I will express gratitude for the lessons that come from different life experiences.

66. Taylor, 17, USA

"Peace: A word that we find in our everyday vocabulary as a word betrayal
A word that was passed down from our ancestors and lost in the midst of the white man
White man ripped the pride out of the native americans and replaced the word peace with war
War against our first people
Treaties broken and words mistaken
Peace
A word that we find in our everyday vocabulary as a word of destruction
A word that has been put in our youth's minds as pills
Our youth hurting because adults don't understand
Pills being shoved down our throat and cut like knives
We are being told this is peace

Peace is not war
Peace is not destruction
Peace is a forest where the breeze flows through your hair
Peace is love
Peace is calm
Peace is not what we have made of it"

Today's intention: I will understand that peace does not have the same meaning to all people. I will go into nature where I can feel peace flowing to me through the breeze.

Nothing is more important than empathy for another human being's suffering. Nothing. Not career, not wealth, not intelligence, certainly not status. We have to feel for one another if we're going to survive with dignity.
Audrey Hepburn

67. Osama, 24, Jordan

"Everyday people can create world peace through acceptance. I believe that acceptance is misunderstood and undervalued. It is misunderstood in that even people who claim to accept others will fold on the first difference in an argument whether it be religious, racial, or even environmental. People also underestimate how hard it can be sometimes to accept others. Still we can make the world a better place for everyone if you were simply capable of accepting differences in our daily life."

Today's intention: When I note a difference with someone today, I will refrain from disagreeing and simply listen. I will strive to understand their perspective.

68. Alejandra, 29, Canada

"It's tied to empathy – understand where the other is coming from. You don't have to agree, but you need to respect each other's opinions. Empathy and respect."

Today's intention: These two words, empathy and respect, will be my mantra for the day. With every encounter I will keep this in mind as I interact with them.

69. Venyhour, 17, Cambodia

"Promoting peace on a small scale is a baby step to establish peace on a bigger scale. Apologies are important in solving a problem. It shows how you understand the situation and how you take responsibility."

Today's intention: What small step can I cultivate into a daily habit to make my life more peaceful? I will choose one small step for today and practice it.

70. Jackie, 47, USA/Australia

"To meditate. Meditate, go within, because then that will make you feel all of that (peace) inside and will bring good energy to the outside world."

Today's intention: I will start my day with 10 minutes of meditation to bring good energy from inside me to the outside world.

First hold peace within yourself, only then can you bring it to others.
Thomas A Kempis

71. Khaila, 17, USA

"I think people can create peace just by being kind to each other. If we all just be kind and not judgmental, there would be less fights, arguments and even bullying. We need to realize that we all have different beliefs and we can't just bash people for them. Another way is raising kids the right way, these things can usually be taught. We should teach the next generation how to be kind, and how to get along with other people and not resort to violence or anger all the time. Something that my theatre arts teacher said that stuck with me was "Assume positive intent", It basically means that when a situation happens we should just assume the other person was doing it in a positive way. I even think that even when they were intentionally doing something negative towards you, they had a positive reasoning behind it even if they did it for themselves or someone else."

Today's intention: I will assume positive intent in the encounters I have with people today.

> *It is not always possible to know why people act the way they do, but I can guarantee that you will feel better if you give people the benefit of the doubt more often than not. When in doubt, be kind. It doesn't cost anything to be kind.*
> **Renee Suzanne**

72. Nnamdi, 24, Nigeria

"I believe everyday people can create peace by understanding, accepting and supporting other people's unique cultures, belief systems, values, and way of life. Live and Let Live!"

Today's intention: I will listen, and not judge, another culture or belief system today. I will be curious about another's way of life.

73. Kristy, 60, USA

"Let's do everything we can to keep the earth vibrating on the highest frequency possible. See the soul not the story. We are all just star dust beings trying to find our way on our trip around this one big star. It's chaos!!! Be kind to everyone including ourselves. Smile. Laugh. Love. " ♥

Today's intention: I will practice kindness with everyone I encounter today, starting with myself.

But each deed you do, each act, binds you to itself and to its consequences, and makes you act again and yet again.
Ursula K LeGuin

74. Rabab, 22, Lebanon

"It is often hard for those who are not at peace with themselves to be at peace with the world or to create peace around them. I believe that everyday people can create peace when they achieve their own inner peace – peace with their thoughts, beliefs, morals, and legacy. Once we understand and reflect on who we are, it becomes easier for us to accept everything around us; the diversity, inequalities, and powers governing our world. This acceptance is the first step towards creating peace. Beyond this acceptance is our own legacy, whether to advocate for world issues or simply to be peaceful with others."

Today's intention: I will reflect on my legacy, beginning with knowing myself and then what role I will play outside myself in the greater world.

75. Somphors, 17, Cambodia

"A few positive words and a smile are all it needs to make peace!"

Today's intention: Even if others are expressing negative thoughts today, I will speak positive words of encouragement.

The world is already so full of conflict. It we want to create more peace in the world, we have to choose not to take things personally and instead respond with understanding, compassion, connection, and peace.
Ben Fizell

76. Gerry, 61, England/France

"You just have to put yourself in the place of the other person. How would I feel if I was treated like this and how should I be justly treated. Treat everyone fairly and they have no cause for hate."

Today's intention: I will consider how I treat others. I choose an intention of fairness and equity in all my dealings for this day.

77. Kayiraba, 29, Cote d'Ivoire/USA

"Everyday people can create peace by cultivating tolerance and acceptance because if we tolerate the difference between cultures, we will be able to understand each other better. Then forgiveness shall be the best way to make people feel better about each other. When we forgive ourselves from the harm we have been doing to other, other people will be able to forgive us in return."

Today's intention: I will forgive myself for a harm I have caused and haven't let go of. I will put it down and move forward.

78. Sovannou, 17, Cambodia

"Life is complicated for every single one of us in this universe. Sometimes we feel happy, sometimes sad or lonely. The only solution for everyone to build peace is that people should be open-minded and forgive each other and this will lead us into living in a beautiful world where everyone is promoting peace."

Today's intention: Today I will focus on someone who has caused me harm that I need to forgive in order to move forward in my life. I will practice forgiveness and promote peace to myself and the other.

79. Alphonce, 40, Tanzania

"What a powerful question! We all need to practice empathy and love towards each other. There seems to be very little of that nowadays. We can practice the art of listening, especially with our children like the 13 year boy."

Today's intention: I will fully listen to what children have to say to me today.

When you talk, you are only repeating what you already know. But if you listen, you may learn something new. **Dalai Lama**

80. Vattey, 17, Cambodia

"Don't force people to agree with what you're saying. Let them decide by themselves. Start from small. Introduce to people what is peace. Not just the definition, but also the feeling and the taste of peace. Let them create their own definition of peace and encourage them to be the change agent who will forward the passage to others, especially the new generation. Last, don't just let people learn and talk about peace, they should also act on those things in real life as well. Tell them, 'make it happen!'"

Today's intention: Be the change you wish to see for peace. Today I will allow someone to disagree with me, instead of needing to be right or needing to convince them. I will allow them to make their own decision based on their beliefs.

81. Alan, 71, United Kingdom

"Try as hard as you can not to make the opposite. I suppose one has to have an arsenal and a strong military, weapons, as a deterrent. But it's also the courage to stand away from others (who are doing the wrong thing). You must love them. You must love them, love others."

Today's intention: I will use my voice to speak up when I see someone doing the wrong thing. I will be an ally for right action.

For things to reveal themselves to us, we need to be ready to abandon our views about them.
Thich Nhat Hahn

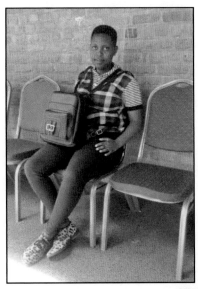

82. Alice, 25, Rwanda

"How people can create peace:
1) Love each other – it's the way of peace,
2) Avoid conflicts,
3) Bring about true equality between women
and men."

Today's intention: I will observe the way I treat women and men differently and commit to equity in my mind and my actions.

❖ There is quantitative evidence that women's empowerment and gender equality are associated with peace and stability in society.

❖ When women influence decisions about war and peace and take the lead against extremism in their communities, it is more likely crises will be resolved without recourse to violence.

❖ A cross national quantitative analysis found that higher levels of female participation in parliament reduce the risks of civil war.

❖ Data on international crises over four decades found that as the percentage of women in parliament increases by five percent, a state is five times less likely to use violence when faced with an international crisis.

www.inclusivesecurity.org
Why Women? Inclusive Security and Peaceful Societies, M O'Reilly, October 2015

83. Kangnaneat, 17, Cambodia

"I think peace goes along with compassion. Forgiving doesn't mean forgetting or giving up; it means we are mature enough to approach the problems in a more ethical way."

Today's intention: Consider what is an ethical approach to creating peace. Does an ethical approach require forgetting or giving in, or can it include forgiveness while continuing to be true to myself and my values? I will think about my personal code of ethics as I interact with others today.

84. Fozia, 37, Pakistan

"Peace is something we have to find in ourselves every day, we can't look for peace outside but the outer world can help us sustain the peace for the longer period of time. We are the source of peace or anger, so keep that in mind when you wake up until you close your eyes at night."

Today's intention: I will note the source of my feelings today - whether in peace or in anger - and choose peace.

85. Mike, 64, USA

"I'm an Oregonian, so not too distant of an opinion. I think there are two words required for World Peace, listening and caring. If people can do this together then understanding of each other can take place. If you think about why people hate others, it is because of cultural histories. Sometimes the listening might involve a reversal of roles to create understanding."

Today's intention: I will think about the cultural history of my country and how I act as a result. I will listen through a cultural lens to another person today so that I can better understand their history and viewpoint.

Rarely are we encouraged to listen carefully and purposefully to other people...listening can be more valuable than speaking. Wars have been fought, fortunes lost and friendships wrecked for lack of listening. It is only by listening that we engage, understand, empathize, cooperate and develop as human beings. It is fundamental to any successful relationship – personal, professional and political.
Kate Murphy

86. Daniel, 39, Ghana

"I think it starts with people loving one another. You see your neighbor as yourself. I think this can bring world peace. When it comes to negotiations on a larger stage, we have to think more about the best solution for all who are involved, and not just what we can get out of it."

Today's intention: I will follow the golden rule, treating others as I would like to be treated. I will think beyond myself to the solution that meets the most needs and not only mine.

87. Sam, 58, USA/Vietnam

"I have been a race director (marathons, triathlons, duathlons, cycling, ultras, 5Ks, etc...) for more than 13 years and have witnessed the power of sports and community. These two forces can be applied to a range of issues, e.g. spiritual connection, raising funds for causes, good health, turning corners on personal issues, and just plain sharing what's in your heart. I have learned that every athlete runs/cycles/swims for a reason. They do so for themselves, a loved one, a cause, or a vision of a better world.

Today's Intention: (Sam's written intention) Go for a run or a bike ride with friends, share your life with them, talk about the future that you want to see. Then, do it again the next day or week until we have peace.

88. Olivier, 38, Rwanda

"It's not just about creating peace among people. It is also important to create peace with nature. I talk daily with people about serious issues and how to get solutions. I have a few close friends, a few best friends, and we share ideas and talk. I talk to them to get advice."

Today's intention: I will connect with one or more friends to exchange ideas about issues affecting our Earth and what steps we can take to create peace with nature.

When despair for the world grows in me
and I wake in the night at the least sound
in fear of what my life and my children's lives may be,
I go and lie down where the wood drake
rests in his beauty on the water,
and the great heron feeds.
I come into the peace of wild things
who do not tax their lives with forethought
of grief.
I come into the presence of still water.
And I feel above me the day-blind stars
waiting with their light.
For a time I rest in the grace of the world,
and am free.
Wendell Berry

89. Maya, 18, Cambodia

"Taking stress and throwing it away, remaining calm, no hesitation. Sharing something that we appreciate with each other. Forgiveness is key to become peaceful, but happiness is when we describe peace."

Today's intention: I will manage my stress so that I may remain calm and bring peace to others.

If you want a calm kitchen, calm your mind.
Suzuki Roshi

90. Kevin, 30, Nigeria

"By paying attention to the little things. By ensuring little misunderstandings do not turn into large problems in the long-run. Such an individual wound would need patience, a cool head and an ability to teach. After all, cooler heads do prevail."

Today's intention: I will pay attention to little misunderstandings, dealing on the spot with any miscommunication. I will keep a cool head.

91. Guy, 62, United Kingdom

"A month ago, I would have said global peace
was an impossibility. However, with the outbreak
of the COVID-19 pandemic, this has become a
universal, unifying dilemma. This disease does not
discriminate by race, religion, sex or wealth. It is
an unseen enemy attacking us all. From what I
can see, a majority of the world's hatred had
shifted from people to a non-living thing, a virus.
People from all countries seem to be putting
aside their differences, uniting to help one
another.

As I work for our National Health Service, I have seen amazing acts of selflessness and kindness. In the United Kingdom, tens of thousands of doctors and nurses have come out of retirement. In one day about a half million people from the general population have volunteered to help. This might be telephoning isolated people or delivering supplies to those who can't leave their homes. I find this outpouring of humanity overwhelming. Perhaps it is a crisis or finding a common goal that helps us all create peace. I'm happy to see that love and compassion can be contagious too."

Today's intention: I will work on a common goal that brings people together to address an issue affecting my community or country. Working with others, I will be part of the solution.

92. Beverly, 68, USA

Part 1: *"Peacemaking is an everyday part of being a nurse. As a nurse, I have the exquisite privilege of caring for people and communities who often feel insecure, anxious, helpless, and afraid – not peaceful. Listening with an open heart in each caring moment can move angst into calm, terror into stillness, and fear into trust. We will both leave the caring moment transformed and at peace."*

Part 2: *"In rural Uganda, in the midst of a camp for people displaced by the civil war, I listened. The participants graphically shared their concerns. Intermittent water supply, scarce food, overflowing toilets, crowded living conditions, etc. As I listened and struggled to understand all that was being shared, one of the women, Ruby, invited me to come see where she was "living" with her three children. I followed, uncertain about what I might encounter, but certain that I wanted to honor Ruby's invitation. We walked through the doorway of the un-fired brick hut. Ruby and I sat next to each other on her small cot and she gifted me the most immense gift. She said, "My heart feels your heart." That's peace."*

Today's intention: I will align my heart with another's today. I will take the time to connect on a personal level.

93. Dalin, 16, Cambodia

"Everyone can seek peace from within. To trigger the peace inside, we need to start by doing small actions every day. Smiling when a stranger passes by, complimenting someone, or initiating a conversation are just some ways to spread positivity, love, and peace.

I believe that peace is equivalent to love. The sentimental sensation you receive from love should feel the same when your mind is peaceful or when you're at peace. Let love lead your conversation, let love speak louder than hate because love is what we want to give and receive."

Today's intention: I will be conscious of giving and receiving love to promote peace.

94. Mary, 30, South Sudan

"Every human-being has the responsibility to help in peace-building by respecting each other, living in social integration, being part of the decision-making in their country, and contributing to the international stability through the local and the international institutions."

Today's intention: I will become informed of the policy issues affecting me on a local, state and national level. I will commit to exercising my right to vote.

95. Sinda, 24, Tunisia

"When thinking of how we can make peace, you'd think of big, complicated words. You would also think of big efforts, right? Peace can, however, be made by assembling little pieces: pieces of love, kindness and of wisdom. Every day people assemble small peaces - empathy, support, mutual respect and small acts of kindness. My pupil once said 'I feel like peace is a dream. It will probably not become a reality, but it is still a sweet dream.'"

Today's intention: I will chunk down the big concept of peace to little pieces (peaces). While I continue to dream that peace is possible, I will take action today in small ways to achieve it.

96. Falk, 45, Germany

"No one in our position can create peace for the other. BUT you can give hope to other people (like I do to take care about the homeless or handicapped people in our region). This won't create peace, but it's one step to make this world a bit better."

Today's intention: I will take one action today that will help those in my community who are less fortunate. I will make the world better through my actions.

97. Tuan, 30, Vietnam

"Starting from October 2018, I have been pushing myself into some daily challenges, such as getting up early in the morning (around 4-5 am), reading great books (30 - 45 minutes), doing physical exercises (25 minutes), reviewing the previous day and creating to-do list for the day. It helps me to better balance my time in order to put my full attention in myself, my family members, my full-time work, as well as my healthy relationships where I can ask for/receive great positive valuable advice every day. So that I can nurture my dreams/goals, provide my son with the good opportunities for his future. I find peace and happiness when I help others."

Today's intention: I will take care of myself first in order that I may help others. I will model healthy behavior.

98. Eman, 21, Libya

"Living in a warzone and with the current security issues that's going on here in Tripoli, I personally believe that art is the middle ground in chaos. I find the only place where people come together and the atmosphere is calm is through art exhibitions that are held in a safer way. I believe it is a way to speak up and get your voice heard and also all people get to enjoy the beauty of it."

Today's intention: I will create or appreciate a piece of art today to foster peace within myself.

99. Karan, 32, Nepal

"For me, people can create peace everyday by not listening to their ego. People focus on the differences between each other and become angry and selfish. Avoiding violence, and by being aware of others, people can create peace."

Today's intention: Today I will look for shared human experiences. Rather than focus on my individual needs, I will act for the common good.

100. Sopheak, 17, Cambodia

"I strongly feel that promoting peace is everyone's obligation. Sometimes we don't even think about the peace that we are maintaining within our everyday life. For example, a minor conflict with a friend could lead you to become a hateful person with a lot of negativity to the world. However, if we come up with solutions that both parties could agree on, that would make the person understand that there will always be positive solutions to conflict which will lead the person to be reasonable and could try to solve problems with a positive attitude which leads to a peaceful resolution. Every day we could start training our brain and everyone around us to always look at any problems in their life with different perspectives, so that they could come up with solutions that would favor both parties."

Today's intention: Today I will train my brain to look at different perspectives; envisioning and working towards a positive outcome.

101. Chris, 36, Denmark

"Being present in all aspects of your waking hours – if it's you socializing, your work, your past time, keeping promises, everything – if you are present you will see the world unfolding in the most spectacular way. And if you are present in everything, you will realise the miracle it is just by you standing here on this earth in this beautiful time."

Today's intention: I will stop, breathe, be present, and appreciate this moment.

You may not always see the results of your kindness, but every bit of positive energy you contribute to the world makes it a better place for all of us.
Lisa Currie

102. Lilly, 31, USA

"Especially during these trying times, I can't help but feel like peace really starts with the individual. I know I struggle to be my best self for others when I don't feel at peace with myself. Peace for me will be when I have finally rid myself of judgment and reactivity, when the most annoying thing in the world doesn't bother me anymore. It seems we have to start with ourselves and then we can begin to focus on the bigger picture; seeing how your own individual peace thread weaves into the larger peace tapestry."

Today's intention: I will refrain from judging others today and I will appreciate the light within them.

103. Namiko, 61, Japan

"Every morning I walk up to the shrine and then go to my work. That's my calm and peaceful time. As for Gaku's question, it's really interesting! I can see how he asked the question to you. (For me, it's) Respect. Consider the reason why the people (she, he, they, we, and I) feel and behave like that."

Today's intention: Every person has a story. I will seek to understand the situation of others today.

104. Heather, 59, United Kingdom

"<u>Sometimes</u> I need to actively resolve the barriers to peace that I've allowed to distance me from peace in the first place, before I can reclaim it again.

<u>Often</u> I can see the beginnings of peace in an object, a place or a person, so need to sit with those feelings a while to let them grow.

<u>Always</u> in mindfulness I can find peace simply in the pause between breathing in and breathing out.

I believe that what you seek with clear intention and action, you will find."

Today's intention: To feel peace, I will practice 4-count breathing. Breathe in 4, hold 4, breathe out 4, hold 4, repeat. I will practice at different times throughout the day.

105. Soumaya, 20, Morocco

- *"Reading books can keep peace with our surroundings, transporting us beyond the demands of daily life.*
- *Physical activity can help to reduce sadness, anxiety and improve our inner peace.*
- *Helping others teaches us that there are people who are in a less healthy situation than ours, and so we value what we have more.*
- *Spending time in nature which can make us have more energy, less sleep disturbances."*

Today's intention: I will choose something to read today that will contribute to my inner peace.

106. Gaynor, 58, England/France

"I create peace by trying to do random acts of kindness whenever I can and standing up when I see discrimination."

Today's intention: When I see discrimination, I will take action to offer support to the target or to address the aggressor.

107. Jean, 94, USA

"I have lived over ninety years. And I think it comes down to kindness. When you go to bed at night, or just at the end of the day, review all of the contacts you have had and ask yourself, "Have you been kind?"

Be kind:

-to yourself

-to everyone you love (and don't love)

And then prepare to do it again tomorrow and the day after that and the day after that...

Kindness matters!"

Today's intention: I will be kind to everyone I meet during this day and tomorrow.

108. Gaku, 16, Japan

"Now (3 years later) I think it's a very difficult question because I have learned about the society we live in. Sometimes there is a very serious gap between an individual's opinion and the public one. I think we have to keep thinking about the situation. We can persist in our opinion, while there are many of other oppositions related to religion, political ways of thinking and so on. It's a very tough action to create a society where we can show respect to each other. To put it simply, we should respect each culture and see unique points of view positively. If my hope comes true, we all will be those who hope for an equal, wonderful, and peaceful world."

Today's intention: Let's be like Gaku, asking hard questions and maintaining hope. How can everyday people create peace?

ACKNOWLEDGMENTS

❖ I first want to thank Gaku – you were the inspiration to keep asking this question and to learn in this way.

❖ To every contributor who shared their responses with me - you are the seeds of thought in this collection.

❖ To the students and staff at the Liger Leadership Academy in Cambodia – for the many gifts you have contributed.

❖ To the MEPI students with whom I have worked and connected – you are the change agents for the MENA region.

❖ To Jaci and her students in western Montana –your heartfelt writing helped me see the many perspectives we hold about peace.

❖ To my Camino Family – for all the support along "the way" and for the bonds of friendship I will forever feel with you. Thanks especially to Kristy who journeyed with me every day.

❖ To my colleagues in peacebuilding – thank you for your on-going commitment to peace and for the lessons we have learned together.

❖ To my artists - cover art and design by Kaitlin Webb (my daughter) and back page art by Gail Brown (my sister). I am so happy to have you as part of this effort.

❖ To Lisa Cox (my Kilimanjaro partner) - for editing with critical eyes and new words, sprinkled with plenty of encouragement.

❖ To Steve, my "QuaranTeam," - you gave me the space to do the writing and editing and weathered the various storms involved in a project like this during a time of great uncertainty.

In deep gratitude, BETSY

GAKU'S CONTRIBUTORS

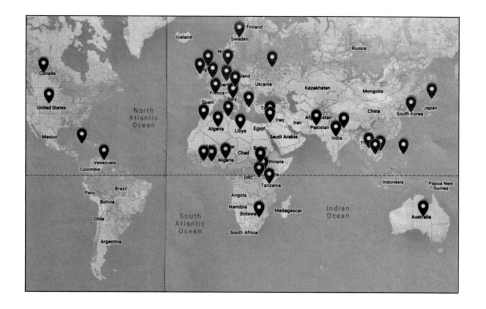

ABOUT THE AUTHOR/EDITOR

Betsy Johnston, LCSW, Ed.D., is a freelance training and organizational development professional with a global reach. Specializing in effective communications, conflict management, leadership development, and community engagement, she has delivered hands-on training to a diverse group of executives, higher education leaders, governmental units, non-profits, community groups, and defense forces.

The peace contributions to this collection come from Betsy's work and travel experiences spanning from 2017-2020. Her work in conflict management training in Africa inspired Gaku at age 13 to ask his question, which became the focal point of this book.

Betsy lives in Bozeman, Montana, USA and has three adult children, Sarah, Kaitlin and Parker, who are each making the world a better place. They share a love for wilderness, travel, new cultures and spicy food.

If you are interested in using Gaku's Question in the classroom or with friends or colleagues, curriculum ideas for K-12 and beyond are available. If you would like to respond to Gaku's question or if you want to learn more about Betsy's availability to work with your organization, you can contact her at **betsy.johnston.j@gmail.com**. To learn more about Betsy's professional history, visit **https://www.linkedin.com/in/betsy-johnston-ed-d-49970625**.

Real peace is when the spirit, the mind, the body, and emotions
Find alignment in our souls
It dances
Swirls
Smiles
And sings
Upon centered feet
With upward hands reaching high for the stars It is not just a thought
Or contentment
But the honoring of our whole being
Where our lives are no longer divided.
Our shadow and light,
Our fears and our joys,
Our uncertainty and our faith
All having a place at the table
Of life.
Peace is not a place of arrival.
But an ongoing weaving of threads
That live in the heart of creation
Of our daily lives.
Peace is verb
More than a noun,
Peace loves deeply,
Even when fear is trying to drive the bus.
Oh won't you come dance with me today
For the world requires more dancing
Than ever before.
Doc Klein 2020

by Gail Brown

Made in the USA
San Bernardino, CA
14 May 2020

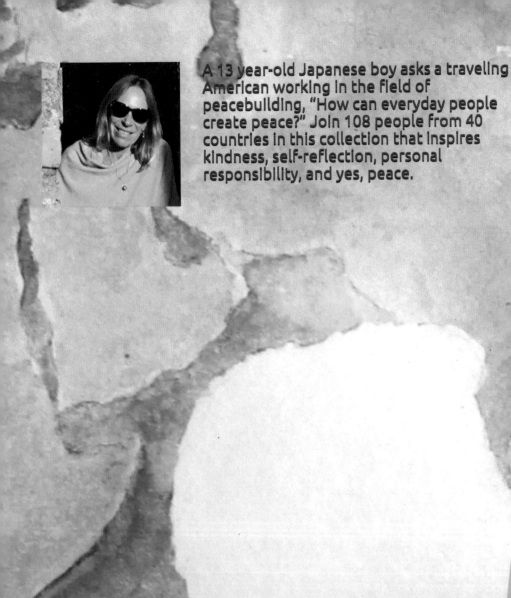

A 13 year-old Japanese boy asks a traveling American working in the field of peacebuilding, "How can everyday people create peace?" Join 108 people from 40 countries in this collection that inspires kindness, self-reflection, personal responsibility, and yes, peace.

ISBN 9798640478709

9 798640 478709

90000